Herbal
TEAS

"Better to be deprived of food for three days, than of tea for one."

Ancient Chinese saying.

Herbal
TEAS

BRENDA LITTLE

A LOTHIAN BOOK

A Lothian Book

THOMAS C. LOTHIAN PTY LTD
11 Munro Sreet, Port Melbourne, Victoria 3207

First published 1994
Copyright © Sandpiper Press (NSW) Pty Ltd 1994

National Library of Australia
Cataloguing-in-publication data
Little, Brenda
Herbal teas.

Includes index.

ISBN 0 85091 650 X.

1. Herbal teas. 2. Herbs. I. Title (Series: Home herbalist).

641.357

A SANDPIPER PRESS PRODUCTION

Published in association with Sandpiper Press (NSW) Pty Ltd
Suite 2, 110 Yarrara Road, Pennant Hills, NSW 2120

Photography by David Liddle

Printed in Australia by Southbank

Contents

Introduction

"I will make you a tisane!" my grandmother would cry, flinging open the door of the cupboard that held her secrets.

You came to Gran when you were too hot, too cold, felt sick and headachy or were just plain tired and grumpy and out of sorts.

"Tisane" was a magic word for me.

It meant being cosseted and comforted and settled in a deep chair to watch while Gran was busy sorting through her collection of exotic little containers. Collecting suitable ones in which to keep her dried herbs was her passion. Each one had to look appropriate for the herb it was to contain.

"That won't do for chamomile!" she once scolded, rejecting the offering of a pretty but highly painted little jar.

Out would come the little blue and white Chinese teapot and the teacups so thin you could see your fingers through them and the ritual began..

"*Chamomillae* for my poor cross girl..." she would say or "*Melissa* for that nasty headache".

She always used the botanical name and that added to the magic. I hated the 'tea' murky with milk that the other grown-ups drank. Grandmother never made "tea"—she made "tisanes".

Into the pot would go two teaspoons of the chosen herb and then we would sit and watch the kettle come to the boil. Her admonitory finger would be lifted as the lid began to tremble and the spout prepared to scream.

"Never ON the boil. Always just OFF the boil."

The water poured into the pot, we sat and waited again.

There was honey in the bee-shaped jar, ready to

put into the steaming drink, and slices of lemon to float on top of it. And there were sponge fingers, crisp and sugary on the outside but which melted in the mouth and sometimes, round little biscuits, so thin the edges were wavy and which tasted of orange. I remember the scents—lime, mint, apple, nutmeg, lemon and rose, and the names. "*Monarda didyma*", which made me laugh, "bee balm", she would then say instead, and "Dew of the Sea" for rosemary and "*achillea*" for yarrow.

I am glad that I have the little blue and white teapot and the fragile cups and a cupboard full of exotic little containers.

A Herb Tea Garden

What did our ancestors in the Western world use as a non-alcoholic drink before travellers brought home from China leaves of the bush that became known as *camellia sinensis* and the long love-affair with "tea" began?

Tea was not known until the mid-sixteen hundreds when Catherine de Braganza, Charles the Second's sad little wife, introduced it to the English Court as an alternative to the intoxicating beverages which were so freely available. The royal patronage ensured that "taking te'" became quite the thing and before long the fashion had ensnared many members of the upper and middle classes. But it was too expensive for poorer people and the tea they drank for comfort and relaxation was made from the leaves and flowers they gathered from the meadows and hedgerows.

There was woodruff—a tiny plant with sweet-scented star-shaped flowers and dark green leaves with strangely hooked edges—meadowsweet, with a froth of fragrant blossom and leaves that dried, carried the scent of new-mown hay—melilot, beloved of the bees, the sweet briar rose. In the "physick" garden they grew herbs for medicines—sage, rosemary, thyme and many more. There was a wide choice of plants from which to make infusions which contained neither tannin nor caffeine but which could brighten a tired and solitary drinker or enliven a social occasion.

Today we think of Indian tea as being "real" tea and anything else as being a departure from the norm. The appellation "herbal tea" sounds vaguely accusing, as though it must be made clear that it isn't all one might think. And "herbal" somehow makes one think of a prescription. How much nicer, now that interest in alternative ingredients for the "cup that cheers" has become so wide, to use the old name 'tisane' which is distinctive and hints at something which is beguilingly different.

In the seventeen hundreds China tea was popular both in England and her American colony to whom she exported it in large amounts. The import tax was heavy and grew heavier and the colonists finally decided they had had enough and refused to let the ships unload their cargo. Tempers flared and over

"Raising herbs for tea is like being warmed twice by firewood: once by cutting and once by burning. First, you can enjoy a host of beautiful and fragrant plants in the garden; later, the same plants offer fragrance and cheer in a cup of steaming herb tea."

three hundred chests of tea were slung into the harbour in an event which became known as the Boston Tea Party and which played a considerable part in provoking the War of Independence.

Deprived of their China tea there was nothing the colonists could do but to fall back on the plants they knew and to experiment with others. It became a matter of national pride to show how well they could do without the wretched stuff. Recipes for what they called Liberty tea, sound very appetising. One called for two parts of raspberry leaves to one part each of bee balm flowers and elderflowers and elderberries. Another for equal parts of wood betony, goldenrod, red clover flowers and leaves of the redroot bush (which I think is a species of *ceanothus*).

It is surely not difficult to be as creative as they were. One can buy from a herbalist dried plants native to other parts of the world and mix them with our own dried garden ones.

Herbs are, on the whole, delightfully good-natured plants, happy to grow among flowers and vegetables and with each other. There are, however some good "haters" among them. I found out the hard way that basil and sage, given the chance, will murder each other, that mint and parsley sulk like mad if forced to share the same bed and that only dill seems willing to put up with having to live near fennel.

They are pleasantly informal plants—they like to sprawl or spread or wander, creating a "sweet disorder" and outwitting all attempts to make them keep themselves to themselves. The amount of work that must have gone into keeping up the formal herb garden of the Middle Ages makes the mind boggle. Few of us today could find the time to maintain such a precise layout and keep the lines clean, clear and orderly, and would we even want to if we could? Gardens which show clearly that man is the boss can be impressive, but are usually short on charm. But what could be more charming than a garden bed where butterflies and bees hover over a wayward spread of herbs lifting their scented leaves and flowers to the sun?

Herbs do not mind a poorish soil, even a dry one, but most of them do like plenty of sun. Many are natives of the Mediterranean area where they struggle

Liberty Tea

Combine equal 2 parts raspberry leaves, elderberries and elderflowers.

Blend the herbs and store in an airtight tin or jar away from the heat or sunlight.

Use by heaping 1 teaspoon of herb mixture for each cup of boiling water. Infuse for 5-10 minutes. Sweeten with honey or maple syrup for an authentic taste.

for life on stony ground and between rocks, under a hot sun and with little to drink. Hardship seems to bring out the best in them for their flavour on their home ground is stronger than when they grow in kinder, gentler conditions. So we don't pamper herbs but we don't treat them all alike either for they do have their preferences.

Which conditions do they like?

Full sun
Basil, bergamot, catmint, lemongrass, parsley, rosemary, sage, thyme

Dappled shade
Angelica, borage, lemon balm, lovage, parsley

Dry conditions
Rosemary, thyme

Moist conditions
Angelica, bergamot, lovage, mint
They don't like having their feet in a puddle though. The soil must be well-drained.

Size and growing habits

When deciding whether to plant herbs among flowers or vegetables or whether to keep them in a bed of their own, mixed or on their own, we have to know a bit about their size and their habits and whether they are annuals or perennials. A few quick lists will come in handy.

Tall herbs
Angelica, goldenrod, lovage, rosemary

Medium sized herbs
Borage, bergamot, lemongrass and sage

Low growing herbs
Basil, catmint, lemon balm, mint, parsley and thyme

Herbs with a spreading growth
Lemon balm, catmint, chamomile, thyme

Herbs with a bushy growth
Lavender, rosemary, sage

Annual herbs
Basil, borage, coriander

Biennial
Angelica

Perennial herbs
Lemon balm, bergamot, chamomile, golden rod, lovage, mint, parsley, rosemary, sage

There are of course many more but the lists are confined to the ones mentioned in this little book.

You could decide, as many people do, to have the upright perennials like angelica, golden rod and lovage growing at the back of the flower border and the low-growing spreading catmint, chamomile and thyme as a front edging. The cheerful little daisy faces of chamomile will not only enliven and decorate the borders of a vegetable plot but the herb will strengthen and protect the crop—the small "plant doctor" is welcome anywhere in the garden.

How about having a small "tea garden" close to the house so that it is easy to nip out and pick a few leaves or flowers to make a quick pot of tea? The herbs that give us pleasant teas to drink are mostly friendly with each other and can be grouped in a special bed.

Two exceptions though. Mint is very thirsty and

an invasive plant and though we want plenty of it, it is best kept in a bed on its own, in part shade, and where it can be watered easily. As large a bed as possible, for mint tea is a great favourite and it is good to have enough to use both fresh and dried. Parsley does well on its own too. It will be picked, not only for making tea but for using for specific cooked dishes so I prefer not to let other herbs encroach on it.

Ordinary soil will do perfectly well for your tea garden. Not too light, not too heavy. And the patch should be weed-free. If you give the soil a thorough going over and get rid of any little oxalis or onion grass bulblets you will do yourself a real favour for they are so difficult to eradicate once they are growing among plants.

A small rectangular bed against a sunny wall or a small, round free-standing bed will hold a surprising number of herbs.

You can grow many of them from seed or save time and propagate from stem or root cuttings. If you inspect your friends gardens carefully you will surely find something you can cajole them into letting you nip off or even divide.

Seedlings, your own grown or bought ones, transplant easily and though you will obviously look after them in the early stages, they will not need the anxious care many flower and vegetable ones demand.

Layering is another method of propagation. I find it works best with the really stout-stemmed plants. A stem from the main plant is bent over to the ground and laid along it. A slight nick in one of the nodal points helps the formation of roots. Soil is heaped over the stem with just a few centimetres of top growth left protruding from the soil. After a few

Layering is the easiest method of propagating herbs. Choose a stem close to the ground. If it is thick make a slanted cut in the underside, put some hormone powder on the cut and bend it down so that you bury it in the soil.

weeks if you carefully scrape away the soil you should find the stem has put out enough roots to enable it to be cut away from the parent plant and to start life on its own.

Garden Pots

Space is not a problem if you want to grow your own herbs. With careful planning a practical herb garden can be grown in pots or hanging baskets. Although clay pots look attractive they do lose moisture more rapidly and need regular water.

If you don't have a real garden you can still have a herb garden for they take very easily to life in a pot.

There are lovely terracotta pots of all shapes and sizes on the market and you can make a spectacular display in the corner of a courtyard or even on a balcony. A portable herb garden has many advantages. You can keep some pots in full sun, give others shade, move them about if a plant looks unhappy or if you get bored with the arrangement.

Mistakes are more easily put right than if the herbs are in the garden proper. You may have given small space to a herb that turns out to be a favourite and find that it is being overgrown by more vigorous ones. The bed is full and extra planting would have to be some distance away. No problem with the pot garden—you just put in an extra pot. When an annual herb dies down, it is far less trouble to whip the pot away, tip it out and replant it with something fresh than to deal with the one growing in the garden bed.

If you are short of space you can very carefully build up pots vertically to about chin height in a widish display.

If you have the space and your climate is right, a linden tree, an elder bush and a hedge of sweet dog roses will extend your tea-making range no end. One hardly thinks of the linden tree as being a herb—it grows about 20m high and has a 10m spread—but if you live in the more temperate parts of the continent, do look around the nurseries for a well-rooted specimen. There are both small and large-leaved varieties and both have scented clusters of pale yellow flowers hanging from a brace. They have a lovely light scent, rather like that of the jonquil and make not only a very refreshing cup of tea for a hot day, but a gentle sedative at the end of a long and tiring one.

The elder is another native of cooler climes, but there are many parts of Australia where it will make a large bush or a small tree. If you know anyone who has one, cadge some cuttings and plant them in the wilder part of your garden—it is not fussy about soil and given adequate sun and water will take and grow quite readily.

Elderflower tea (30g flowers to a litre of near boiling water) is pleasant enough and good to drink if you feel a cold coming on but, for me, the real joy is

the champagne you can make from those scented flowers! It is quite simple to make and guests thoroughly appreciate being offered a glass or two as an alternative to cups of tea.

This recipe uses fresh flowers.

Elderflower Champagne

Ingredients

> 2 good handfuls elderflowers
> 700 g sugar
> 1 lemon
> About 4 litres of water
> 2 tablespoonfuls white vinegar

Method

1. Grate the lemon rind, squeeze the juice
2. Add to the elderflowers, sugar and vinegar. Stir, 3. Add water and stir again.
4. Cover the container—preferably a large glass or china dish or enamelled saucepan. Do not use an aluminium container.
5. Leave to stand for at least 24 hours.
6. Strain carefully, twice if necessary, and bottle, using corks well hammered in or screw tops.
7. Leave in a dark place for at least 3 weeks before opening.

The dog rose *rosa cauina* or as you may know it, the briar rose, has flowers with a lovely, simple old-fashioned face. The five delicate petals are sweetly scented. A handful picked as you pass will make a pleasant cup of tea.

The rose gives full value. The dried leaves can be used for tea too and everybody knows about the valuable vitamin C the oval rose-red "hips" contain. They dry very easily and make an astringent cuppa, but are mostly used in conjunction with other herbs. A favourite commercial blend is rosehip with hibiscus.

Watch out for the irritant hairs if you try using the hips fresh. Because of the need to strain the tea so well, most people prefer to use the dried hips.

Making Herbal Tea

Herb teas are flavourful, refreshing
and can positively contribute to
health. They do not contain tannin,
caffine or fluoride, but have properties that
can soothe, refresh, and invigorate; many are
so mild in their therapeutic properties that
they can be given to children. Altogether they
make a valuable contribution to the diet if
taken on a regular basis.

It is a real joy to nip out into the garden, cut off a few leaves from a green and healthy plant, and, no more than ten minutes later, be sitting down enjoying a fragrant cup of tea made from them.

"Fresh" is a lovely word. The dictionary says it means "retaining the original properties unimpaired". The fresh herbs give us the very best of themselves in that clear, clean liquid.

Tastes vary. Some people like weak tea, some like it strong so it is as well to experiment a bit. Herbs taken straight from the garden can have a stronger taste than ones bought at the market and kept in the frig for a few days. One to two teaspoonsful of fresh, well-chopped herb to one cup of near boiling water is a useful yardstick. I tend to be overgenerous with the herb on the grounds that if you find the tea too strong you can always dilute it and feed the surplus to thirsty pot plants, but you can't do much with a wishy-washy brew.

The teapot I use when making a pot just for myself holds 600mls water, enough for about three cups of tea.

I use three good heaped teaspoonsful of fresh herbs to a full pot and let it stand for five minutes. When I pour out the first cup, I top up the pot.

This is left to stand while I relax and enjoy doing nothing at all but sitting quietly, sipping and thinking.

The tea is still hot enough when I need a second cup.

The remainder is left in the pot to go cold. It provides a pleasant drink later on. Any left is fed to the plants or compost heap.

A friend calls all this my "funny little ways" but you should see my pot plants.

Some people enjoy the taste of the tea "neat". Others like the addition of honey and lemon. Again it is a matter of experimentation. Herbs such as lemon thyme and lemon verbena have their own clean and pleasant taste and need no additives but others can be improved by them.

Using dried herbs

If you buy commercial herb tea sachets the instructions come with them.

Ensure that your teas are kept in an airtight container to preserve the flavour.

Home-dried herbs are usually quite strong and little more than half a teaspoonful per cup or 25g to a 600ml pot will do. But there are no hard and fast rules as strength can vary from one drying to another. I find too that if you are using blend of herbs the strength of one of them will predominate from brew to brew. The results though variable are always pleasing.

The important thing when making herb tea is to put the teapot lid on firmly so that the essential oils are not carried away in the steam.

It is best to use a pot even when making just one cup of tea. You can buy some very pretty little ones.

Some people use infusers when making just one cup but an infuser doesn't always hold the amount of fresh herb necessary and its shape doesn't allow the cup to be covered to keep in the steam.

Drying concentrates the flavour of a herb considerably so you will always need less by weight, though not by bulk, of the fresh herb.

I don't find judgement the old maxim for ordinary tea—"one for each nob and one for the pot" works very well for me so I am hesitant about giving precise amounts. As said before, much depends on individual taste and also the way the herb was gathered and stored. The bought one-cup sachets are usually too strong for me and I can make three cups out of one. Other people could find the taste woeful.

If when you first begin to experiment with herbal teas and you don't find them as flavoursome as you would like, try them mixed with a little China,

A Glossary of Tea Terms

Decoction: *A beverage made by simmering herbs for 10-20 minutes. This method is generally used to bring out the full flavour of roots and seeds and for some flowers and leaves such as lemon verbena.*

Flavoured tea: *Tea which has been flavoured, usually with essential oils of fruits, spices or herbs.*

Green tea: *China tea that has been dried but not oxidised or fermented.*

Infusion: *A beverage made by pouring boiling water over herb leaves or flowers and steeping them for 5-10 minutes to release the aromatic oils. A general recipe is 1 teaspoon of dried herb or 3 teaspoons of fresh, crushed herbs per cup of boiling water. For a stronger drink add more herb but don't steep the tea longer as this may cause the tea to become bitter.*

You use an infuser to steep the herb. This is a small perforated metal ball used to hold the tea leaves while they steep in the hot water.

Sun tea: *Tea made by adding tea leaves to cold water in a lidded glass jar and leaving in full sunshine for 4 to 8 hours. The sun warms the water and causes the gentle release of the aromatic oils. Teas made by this method have a very smooth flavour and rarely turn cloudy in the refrigerator, as steeped teas sometimes do.*

Tisane: *An infusion, originally of barley but now usually of fresh or dried herbs; used as a beverage or medicinal tea.*

If when you first begin to experiment with herbal teas and you don't find them as flavoursome as you would like, try them mixed with a little China, Jasmine or Earl Grey tea—not a lot, just enough to make the presence felt. Raspberry and strawberry teas give added flavour too but they contain tannin.

Chamomile, mint, lemon balm, lemon verbena, lemongrass, lime, sage, rosemary, thyme, rose hip, bergamot, catmint, hyssop are all aromatic plants which make pleasant teas, but not all sweet-smelling ones do. The geranium leaves which carry the scent of apple or nutmeg are not nice at a—the rose geranium holds its scent though, perhaps a little too well for a cup of tea on its own. A leaf or two in blends of other teas can be very pleasant.

In the summer a large pot of tea made in the morning can be left to go cold and made into a long, cooling drink with the addition of ice-cubes or some sparkling mineral water.

Incidentally I have recently used frozen herbs to make a pot of tea. I had no fresh parsley or lemon-grass but had some little bundles of them wrapped in foil stored in the freezer. The tea tasted fine but I don't know how its properties were affected.

Infusers are used to steep the herb. They hold leaves or herb mixtures while the hot water moves through the holes. Don't infuse too long or the tea may become bitter.

Tea Herbs

These few easy-to-grow herbs made a good basis for a "tea garden". There are mild "tea-time" herbs and "lunch-time" ones which have a more savoury flavour.

ALFALFA

Medicago sativa   *pilionaceae*

Although better known as a field crop or as sprouted seeds bought in a little tray from greengrocers and supermarkets, you could grow a patch of alfalfa in the garden. It is a perennial which grows to about a metre high, with small bright-green leaves and little lilac-violet flowers.

Tea can be made from leaves, stems and flowers and, while it is not strongly or particularly pleasantly flavoured, the plant is so packed with goodness that it would be a shame to ignore it. You can use it fresh or dried and mixed with other herbs. Peppermint goes well with it. You may know it better as lucerne hay so will be able to imagine the faintly sweet earthy taste of the tea.

Farmers have been feeding their stock on it for years—it keeps them healthy and fattens them up; athletes drink it for added stamina and mothers to keep up their supply of breast milk. Alfalfa sprouts also contain oestrogen, but one would have to eat it in great quantities to replace the natural decrease of this hormone in women who are approaching the end of their child bearing years!

Cultivation
Sow from seed if you can get it or try planting out a bought tray of sprouts.

ANGELICA

Angelica archangelica   **Apiaceae**

This is one of the tallest herbs and, at the back of the border, can reach 2 metres in height.

It is biennial with glossy green leaves, crisp hollow stems and umbels of sweet-scented yellowish-white flowers which are followed by large seed-heads. The whole plant carries a sweet, clean scent—see if you can detect it when you next drink vermouth or Chartreuse.

Tea made from the leaves has a high sugar content, a not unpleasant taste and is a "soother" both of nerves and stomach. If you don't care for it straight, add the dried leaves to a mixture of other herbs and at least get the benefit of its therapeutic properties. You can also make tea from the stems, seeds and dried root.

While not exactly a plant to provide a tea for social occasions, angelica is a useful "teatime" one because the stalks can be candied and used for decorating cakes. If you have a guest troubled by flatulence, offer a small fresh piece of stalk to be chewed—it tastes nice, is warming to the stomach and does away with social embarrassment!

Cultivation

Plant at the back of the border in good soil and a little shade, allowing each plant good all-round space. Keep well watered. The plants self-seed easily.

BASIL

Ocimum basilicum   *Lamiaceae*

I doubt if you would want to grow basil especially for making tea, although it does taste quite nice with a slice of orange in it, but one or two good healthy plants of sweet basil grown in a pot will come in handy for making a basil and borage tea. Always use the herbs fresh, not dried. This tea is especially good when you feel low and too tired to move. You can juggle with the amount of herbs used—basil has the stronger flavour.

Cultivation
Keep your pots of basil in a warm spot and water freely and regularly.

BERGAMOT
(BEE BALM, OSWEGO TEA)

Monarda didyma   *Lamiaceae*

This is a splendid garden plant, a perennial which, given plenty of water, will grow to over a metre high. It has large, oval, slightly hairy, toothed leaves, shaggy, showy flower heads, from mauve to rich red in colour. The tubular flower petals are full of nectar so this is a great plant for bringing bees to the garden. Both leaves and flowers have a fresh strong fragrance.

The plant's familiar name of Oswego Tea was given to it by early settlers in America who found that the Osweg Indians made a beverage from it. They were happy to follow suit.

Tea made from the leaves and flowers tastes a bit like a strongly scented China tea, and is as good cold as it is hot.

It makes a good soporific too so can make a change from hot milk at bedtime. If you have made a mixture of teas which seems a bit flat, add a few bergamot flower-heads to liven it up.

Cultivation

Sow seeds in boxes and plant out in the Spring. Bergamot likes a rich, moist soil where the roots can stay cool, so keep at the back of the border in part shade.

It makes a good solid plant which can be propagated by root division and is best divided every few years.

BORAGE

Borago officinalis   *Boraginaceae*

Bees love borage and a delightful plant it is too. The star-shaped flowers are pale and pinkish in bud but turn to a clear, quite startling "Madonna" blue.

The black anthers which protrude from them are covered with pollen.

It is a good plant to grow in a "tea" garden if only for the pleasure of having the flowers to candy.

If you brush the freshly opened flowers with white of egg and dust them with caster sugar, you can either leave them to dry naturally on waxed paper or put them in a slow oven and then use them as cake decoration.

Since the flowers can be eaten raw they can be added to a salad or a dish of fruit or ice-cream.

If you drop a fresh flower into each section of the freezer tray you can have flower-filled ice-blocks to decorate long summer drinks.

The stems and leaves bristle with hairs which can be uncomfortable to touch, so the leaves, which have a pleasant cucumber taste, should only be used in salads or cool summer drinks when they are young and tender and before the hairs have developed strongly.

Borage does not dry well—the flavour and goodness is lost so both flowers and leaves are best used fresh.

A tea made from the leaves and flowers is rich in calcium and potassium. It makes a good tonic and blood cleanser and is not only exhilarating but can promote the flow of breast milk.

In the old days borage was known as "the herb of courage". and was said to "drive away all sadness". Modern research has found that it can stimulate the adrenaline glands so the name is not far wrong.

A pot of tea made from a mixture of basil and borage leaves has a distinctly pleasant taste.

Cultivation

The annual grows tall and can reach nearly a metre in height. It likes well-drained soil, moisture and protection from strong sun. Since the plant tends to

droop it is seen at its best when massed and protected from the wind.

It grows easily from seed, and once in the garden
is likely to be a permanent guest for it self-seeds
readily.

CATMINT/CATNIP

Nepeta cataria   *Lamiaceae*

Tea made from the leaves and flowers was made before "tea" was introduced from the East.

With its heart-shaped grey-green leaves and pale lavender flowers it makes a pretty perennial border plant. Both flowers and leaves give off a delicate fragrance. As is obvious from its name cats love it. I was told they are not so keen on the smaller *nepeta mussini* but I find that our cat is out like a flash once I cut either type and the scent is fully released.

The taste of tea made from the fresh herb is definite but the dried leaves give a tangier one. Always gather young leaves and the young flowering plant tips.

The plant is rich in Vitamin C and makes a good tea for children as it is good for the digestion and fractiousness. It is also a good one to drink when you feel a cold coming on.

Cultivation

The old saying "if you set it, the cats will eat it, if you sow it the cats won't know it", is worth remembering. They go for transplants, no doubt because handling has released the scent. An initial sowing is all that is needed, once in the garden the plants self-seed readily.

Catmint likes the sun but can tolerate shade, and is not too fussy about soil, but does need adequate water. It is something of a straggler and will need a little control.

CHAMOMILE

Anthemis nobilis   *Asteraceae*

The Egyptians dedicated this little plant to the sun and worshipped it. Greek physicians used it and the Anglo-Saxons included it in their list of nine sacred herbs so it has a long provenance of usefulness. Gardeners used to call it the "plant doctor" because sick plants growing near it would revive.

Tea made from the little golden flowers, fresh or dried, is a great reviver of tired people too and is now widely used not only as a tonic and a soother of the over-stressed and restless but just for the pleasure of its clean and individual taste.

It is a low creeping little perennial with feathery, apple-scented leaves and flowers like small white daisies with a cushiony yellow centre. The flowers should be picked for making tea when they are fully open.

It is surprising to find that such a little plant can offer so much—it can be used cosmetically, medicinally, as a dye and as part of a pot-pourri, so space should always be made for plenty of it in the garden.

Cultivation

You can grow it from seed, from cuttings or by dividing an established plant. It likes full sun and a light, well-drained soil.

When you pick flowers for tea, you can tidy the plant up by trimming the leaves and drying them for use in pot-pourri.

GOLDEN ROD

Solidago odora　　　　　　　　　　***Asteraceae***

This is one of the plants the American colonists used for making tea, probably even before the Boston Tea party deprived them of China tea. When I lived in England it was a flower I was always sorry to see appear in the border, for along with the Michaelmas daisies, it heralded the end of summer. It is a tall plant—the stems are crowned with clusters of sweet, golden flowers which wave in the breeze and look very attractive.

Tea made from the blossoms is said to have an aniseed taste and to be good for the digestion. I haven't tried it yet but since it is still drunk in America it must be good!

Cultivation

It grows from seed quickly and well. It has a healthy appetite and the soil in which it grows should be quite rich and kept well fed and well watered. The plant can look stringy otherwise.

LEMON BALM

Melissa officinalis   ***Lamiaceae***

This easy-to-grow perennial spreads wonderfully and can be kept tidy by a constant picking of the stems and leaves. The leaves are rough and crinkled, a bit like nettles and give off a strong and very pleasant lemony scent. Used fresh it makes a very clean and refreshing tea—something seems to be lost when the leaves are dried, although they hold their scent quite well.

Melissa tea has been a favourite down the centuries—it was said to prolong life and to lift depression. "Heart's delight" was one of its names.

It is certainly one of the nicer-tasting herb teas, particularly when sweetened with honey. Try floating a leaf or two on the top of a cup of Indian tea without milk, of course.

Cultivation

Lemon balm likes sun, not too hot and can take some shade, is not fussy about soil as long as it is well-drained and well-watered. It can be grown from seed, cuttings and by plant division.

It makes a spreading bushy plant. As its botanical name suggests it is a "bee" herb and is a good plant to have in the garden on that account alone.

LEMON GRASS

Cymbopogon citratus   *Poaceae*

The tall reed-like leaves of the lemongrass look good in the garden when the plant is growing strongly and make a delightful drink which is as nice cold as hot. Because they cut up so neatly they are very easy to use fresh and emptying the pot is cleaner and quicker than when other herbs are used.

The plant is a perennial but you can't always count on it—if it gets too cold or too dry, it packs it in. It dies down in winter and struggles it sway up again when the ground and the air have really warmed up in spring and doesn't look at its best until high summer. But it can be forgiven everything for the profusion of the clump when it does get going and for the truly delicious taste of the tea made from its leaves. Tip any tea left over into the bath!

Its flavour may very well be familiar to you if you frequent Thai restaurants.

The leaves dry quite well and can be used to liven up the taste of other less flavoursome brews.

Cultivation

Given good soil, warmth and regular, plentiful watering it can do very well indeed. Increase by division.

LEMON VERBENA

Aloysia triphylla   ***Verbenaceae***

The pale green pointed leaves of this bushy little shrub have a delicious lemony taste and used, fresh or dried, alone or mixed with mint leaves, make a good tea. It is a bit sharper than the other lemon-flavoured herbs—more like the flavour of the rind than the juice. It is a good tea to drink while sitting talking after a meal—particularly if the meal was heavy.

Many dried herbs lose their potency and scent after 6 months or so but lemon verbena seems able to retain them for much longer.

The leaves have their best flavour just when the flowers are opening.

Cultivation

This is one herb of the herbs which need to be kept fairly dry and the soil need not be rich either. It makes quite a sizeable perennial shrub which drops its leaves at the end of the season. It can over-winter without trouble in temperate areas but will need protection where there are frosts and snow. It doesn't mind being cut well back as long as it is covered. Straw will protect it and rot down and provide nourishment.

Propagation is from cuttings taken from new wood.

MINT

Mentha   *Lamiaceae*

Both peppermint and spearmint make excellent teas—the apple, basil, ginger and pineapple, I have found disappointing and the eau-de-cologne mint is, as it sounds, a herb to use cosmetically.

Peppermint has a stronger taste than spearmint. The leaves can be used, fresh, dried or mixed with other herbs.

I have heard it said that drinking mint tea too often will irritate the mucous membranes but have never found anyone who complained of it.

Since it is such a widely used culinary herb it is very useful to have a big bed of mint.

The leaves should be picked, on the stem, before flower-buds have had time to form and care should be taken not to bruise them before using either fresh or dried.

I grew up believing it unwise to drink peppermint tea after four o'clock in the afternoon as if you did, you would not sleep well that night.

When I bought a packet of tea for sleeplessness recently I found that one of the ingredients was spearmint. The others were chamomile, lemongrass and passionflower leaves. With Gran in mind I haven't got around to trying it yet.

Cultivation

Mint likes more shade and moisture than most other herbs and, since it is highly invasive, is better when given a cool spot all to itself. It never seems to do well in a bed of mixed herbs and it positively hates being grown anywhere near parsley.

The soil should be light and loamy.

The plant roots are vigorous and "travel". You can safely chop off a section of plant and resite it elsewhere.

All herb teas can be enjoyed when cold, with or without ice. Mint leaves, thyme leaves, borage flowers etc make delicious additions.

Lunch-time Herbs

Some herbs have a robust flavour more suitable to lunch than tea-time. Tea made from these herbs is good with a salty biscuit and a sliver of cheese.

PARSLEY

Petroselinum crispum   *Apiaceae*

Parsley tea made with freshly cut leaves and given a touch of salt and ground pepper is a good mid-morning warmer and stimulant, rich in vitamins and minerals and a good alternative to a cup of Bonox.

It is worth a try made with dried parsley, but only if it still holds its colour.

Cultivation

Parsley likes good rich soil in full sun or light shade. It grows well from seed sown in Spring or seedlings. Since then seed has a tough coating it helps to soak it in water overnight. Once you have it in the garden you can allow a few plants to self-seed, which they will do very willingly.

LOVAGE

Levisticum officinale   *Apiaceae*

Lovage leaves have a strong savoury taste, a bit like celery, a bit like parsley but with a peppery yeasty bite. I would say that a beverage made from them is likely to be an acquired taste but since lovage is a good herb to grow for cosmetic purposes and since the leaves make an interesting soup and a good deodorising bath herb, you are likely to want to grow the herb and will have the leaves with which to experiment. They dry quite well.

Lovage is a handsome plant, not unlike angelica but does not grow quite as tall. The leaves are dark-green, toothed and deeply serrated, the flowers small and insignificant, the stems like those of angelica are hollow and can be chewed but their flavour is hardly conducive to candying.

Cultivation

It needs a rich soil, regular watering and will grow well in either full sun or partial shade. Given an all round space of about 50cm it makes a useful back-of-the-border plant.

It is not difficult to grow from seed, but root-cuttings are quicker. It is a good self-seeder.

ROSEMARY

Rosmarinus officinalis   ***Lamiaceae***
The young at our place reject rosemary tea on the grounds that it tastes like disinfectant and are not cajoled by the promise that it is renowned for assisting the memory and that students of ages gone by have blessed its name. Those of us more worried about our memory could develop quite a taste for the tea which is brisk, astringent and warming. It is not a tea to be sweetened or accompanied by little biscuits, but one to be drunk on its own.

The tiniest touch of Vegemite on the end of a spoon adds to the taste as does a mixture of rosemary and lemon-balm or lemongrass.

You can use the leaves either fresh or dried. Since the herb is strong-tasting, you don't need much.

Cultivation

Since it is a native of the Mediterranean region, rosemary can take both heat and dry soil but hates having its roots "puddled" so make sure the soil drains well. It can be grown as a hedge or border edging but will have to be kept trimmed. As a single specimen—and the bushes are quite large—it can be left to find its own shape.

Propagation is easiest from cuttings or root division.

SAGE

Salvia officinalis   *Lamiaceae*

Everyone seems to have sage in the garden. It is the cook's herb and its dry pungent flavour and sharp tang is welcome for the way it "cuts" fatty foods. There are many varieties of sage and some have a stronger flavour than others. Purple sage makes a very strong tea—the variegated ones and the narrow-leaved one, *salvia lavendifolia*, make the nicest ones.

Two good reasons for trying sage tea is that the herb has a long reputation for helping to prolong life and to restore the memory. Add to that, any tea left in the pot can be used as a rinse to stop the hair turning grey and the regular rubbing of a sage leaf over the teeth will keep them pearly white. It is obvious one cannot afford not to have sage in the garden.

It makes an attractive bush—the young leaves are the palest green but turn silver-grey as they mature—the mauvish-purple flowers are lipped and deep-throated and beloved of bees.

Cultivation

Sage is not particular about soil, likes sun and being kept on the dry side.

Whenever you water make certain it all drains away as the plant, like most silvery-leaved ones hates having its feet left wet.

The bush can get untidy and needs pruning to keep in shape.

Propagation can be from seed but its quicker and easier to use cuttings.

THYME

Thymus   **Lamiaceae**

There are several varieties of thyme—the ones to grow for tea making are the common garden thyme and the lemon thymes.

If you grow other varieties for their decorative value (Westmoreland, Silver Posie, *aureus* and the woolly thyme) plant them well away from your tea herbs so you won't get them confused.

Common thyme is a small bushy perennial with

small, narrow grey-green leaves which grow on wiry stalks off the main stems and small pale pinkish-lilac flowers—the lemon thymes have broader leaves. They are all strongly aromatic and can be used fresh or dried.

The Greeks called the plant "thymus"—which is derived from their word "Thymon" which means 'courage' and it certainly makes a vitalising tea.

The strength of the tea will be a matter of taste and some experimentation may be needed. Try honey and lemon with the common thyme and a few lavender flowers with the lemon ones.

Cultivation

The scent of thyme crushed underfoot—how evocative that strange sweetness can be. Since it is low-growing it will naturally be grown at the front of the border and will be forgiven if it strays onto the path.

Thyme likes poor soil and hot sun—the conditions of its natural habitat, the Mediterranean region, and does not like the cold. If you cut it back at the end of the season do give it a bit of protection to see it through the winter. You could then lift a plant and let it winter indoors. Although a perennial it is only at its best for two years, so be prepared to replace it then.

Propagation is from heeled cuttings or root division.

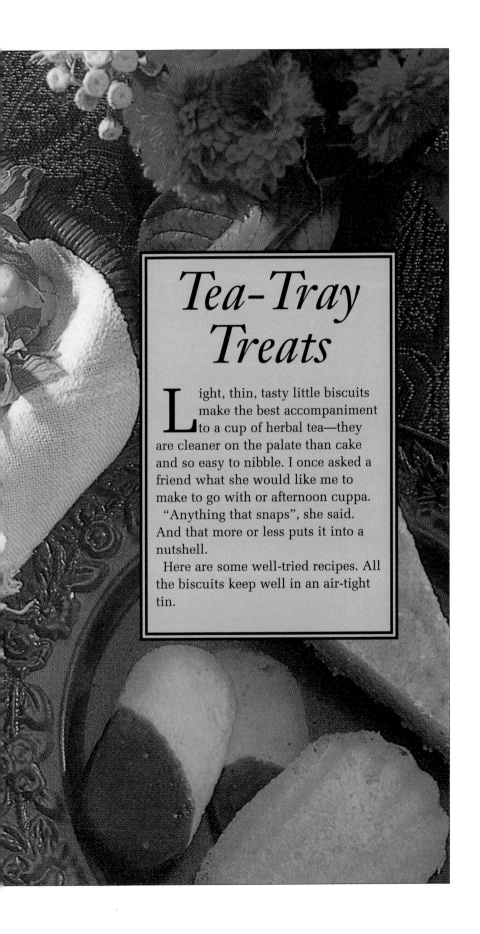

Tea-Tray Treats

Light, thin, tasty little biscuits make the best accompaniment to a cup of herbal tea—they are cleaner on the palate than cake and so easy to nibble. I once asked a friend what she would like me to make to go with or afternoon cuppa.

"Anything that snaps", she said. And that more or less puts it into a nutshell.

Here are some well-tried recipes. All the biscuits keep well in an air-tight tin.

SHORT BREAD

Good plain short bread—imagine a piece with steaming hot chamomile tea.

Ingredients
Half cup butter
Half cup brown sugar
2 cups sifted plain flour
Dash of salt (optional)

Method
1. Cream butter until light and fluffy
2. Add sugar and beat until dissolved
3. Work in flour and salt. Mixture will be dry.
4. Divide dough into 2 parts and press each half firmly into the bottom of a pan (about 22cm)
5. Prick with fork at 30mm intervals
6. Bake in the oven at 160 degrees C for 25 to 30 minutes. Cut pieces through while warm.

VANILLA WAFERS WITH CHOCOLATE GLAZE

Mint and chocolate are a classic combination but a refreshing cup of mint tea wants only a little chocolate, slightly bitter.

Ingredients
Three quarters cup butter
Half cup sugar
1 egg yolk
Half tspn vanilla
2 cups sifted plain flour

Method
1. Cream butter and sugar
2. Stir in egg yolk and vanilla
3. Gradually add flour and mix well
4. Chill dough until easy to handle
5. Form into 2 flattened rolls 4cm in diameter before flattening
6. Wrap in wax paper and chill for 2 hours
7. Pre-heat oven to 200 degrees C
8. Cut dough into 3mm slices and bake for 8 minutes or golden brown
9. Cool. Dip half of each biscuit in chocolate glaze.

Chocolate glaze
170g semisweet chocolate pieces
2g bitter chocolate
Quarter cup milk
Melt chocolate pieces together in a double boiler
over boiling water. Add milk and stir until smooth.

WHEATGERM THINS

Ingredients
Half cup oil
1 cup brown sugar
1 egg
3 tablespoons milk (cow or soya)
1 cup wheatgerm
2 cups wholemeal flower
(OR one and a half cups wholemeal flour and half
cup soya flour)
1 tspn vanilla essence
Half tspn salt

Method
1. Cream oil and sugar.
2. Add the milk, vanilla, salt, wheatgerm and beaten
egg. Mix well.
3. Shake in the flour to make a stiff dough.
4. Shape the dough into a roll – Swiss roll size.
5. Wrap it in greaseproof paper and leave it in the
frig. overnight.
6. The next day heat the oven to 180 degrees C.
7. Unwrap the dough and cut into thin slices.
8. Spread slices out on a baking sheet and cook until
brown and crisp, approximately 15 to 20 minutes.

RICE BIKKIES

Ingredients
1 cup rice flour
Quarter cup sugar
Half cup soft butter
1 beaten egg
1 tspn almond essence
Half tspn baking powder
1-2 tspn water

Method
1. Mix all ingredients together and form into a ball.

2. Flatten out with a rolling pin, not TOO thinly, and, using a cutter, make into rounds.

3. Place a blanched almond on the top of each biscuit, glaze each one with milk.

4 Cook, spread out on a baking tray, for 20 minutes in a moderate oven (180 degrees C)

ORANGE COCONUT CRISPS

Ingredients
125g butter
155g sugar
1 beaten egg
250g self-raising flour
90g desiccated coconut
Grated orange rind.

Method
1. Cream butter and sugar
2. Add beaten egg and orange rind. Mix well.
3. Add flour and coconut. Mix again.
4. Make dough into small balls.
5. Coat in any remaining coconut.
6. Spread out over a baking tray and cook for 20 minutes in a moderate oven (180 degrees C.)

WALNUT ROUNDS

Ingredients
3 egg whites
150g plain flour
150g caster sugar
160g shelled walnuts

Method
1. Beat egg whites until stiffish.
2. Add sugar, beating as you go. Beat until mixture is stiff.
3. Very gently sift the flour into the mixture
4. Add the walnuts and stir in, again very gently.
5. Lightly grease a Swiss roll tin or any narrow longish tin or glass dish.
6. Spoon the mixture into the container. Do this slowly and steadily. When done pat the outside of the container smartly to get rid of any air bubbles.
7. Cook in a moderate oven (180 degrees C) for

around forty-five minutes. The mixture should be firm to the touch.

8. Leave to stand until cold.

9. Remove mixture carefully, wrap in aluminium foil and leave in the frig overnight or even longer.

10. Now comes the tricky part.
Using a finely serrated knife, cut the mixture into very thin slices.
Spread out on an oven tray and bake in a slow oven for 20 minutes. When they are done they should be crisp and slightly changed in colour.

11. Don't store in a tin until completely cold.

Lunchtime nibbles

CHEESEY BISCUITS

Ingredients
    60g butter (margarine if you must)
    60g cheddar or other sharp cheese, finely grated
    Half cup plain flour
    1 egg
    1 tspn curry powder
    Sesame seeds
    Good shake of salt

Method
1. Cream butter, add egg yolk, beat together.
2. Add grated cheese. Mix well.
3. Add flour and salt and mix until a firm dough.
4. Roll into a ball and leave in the frig for at least half an hour.
5. Roll out thinly and cut into small rounds.
6. Place on a greased baking tray.
7. Beat up the white of egg and paint each biscuit with it.
8. Mix together curry powder and some sesame seeds and sprinkle over the biscuits.
9. Bake at 200 degrees C. for 12 to 15 minutes.
10. Leave until cool before storing in a tin.

CHEESE BALLS

Ingredients
    125g grated cheese

185g butter
One and a half cups plain flour
Salt and pepper
1 tspn paprika
2 tablespoons sesame seeds.

Method
1. Cream butter, add cheese, work in flour, salt and pepper.
2. Make into small balls. Roll in sesame seeds.
3. Bake in moderate oven (180 degrees C.) for 12 minutes.

CHEESE SNAPS

Ingredients
2 eggs
Three quarter cup milk
2 cups self raising flour
1 cup grated cheese

Method
1. Beat eggs in milk.
2. Add flour and cheese. Mix.
3. Roll out fairly thinly and cut into strips.
4. Cut strips into biscuit lengths and place on a greased baking tray.
5. Bake at 200 degrees C until brown.
6. Take out of oven and split each biscuit in two lengthways.
7. Rearrange on sheet and return to oven until the cut side has browned.

CHEESE STRAWS

Ingredients
60g butter
90g grated cheddar cheese
One and a quarter cups plain flour
1 egg
One and a half tablespoons lemon juice
Salt and pepper
Sesame seeds (optional)

Method
1. Rub butter into flour until it is like breadcrumbs.
2. Add grated cheese with salt and pepper.

3. Mix together.
4. Separate the egg.
5. Mix yolk with the lemon juice.
6. Make well in the centre of the mixture
7. Add egg and lemon juice and mix into a firm dough.
8. Roll out thinly into a neat rectangle. Neaten the edges.
9. Use a sharp knife and cut the pastry into long strips about 5mm wide.
10. Cut strips into 10cm lengths. Place carefully on an oiled baking tray.
11. Beat white of egg fairly stiffly and brush each 'straw' with it.
12. Place carefully on a well-oiled baking tray and bake for 12 minutes in a moderate oven. (180 degrees C.).
13. Do not allow the 'straws' to become too brown— they will be done when they become pale gold.

For something more substantial, try Beer Bread with some cheese and sliced onion.

BEER BREAD

Ingredients
    3 cups self raising flour
    1 tablespoon sugar
    1 tspn salt
    1 can Tooheys Old Beer (small)

Method
1. Sift flour and salt.
2. Add sugar. Mix in.
3. Add beer and blend—lightly.
4. Spoon into a well-oiled loaf tin and bake at 200 degrees C. for 45-50 minutes.
5. Loaf is done when it sounds hollow when rapped.

Pancakes with thyme butter (chopped herb beaten into some butter) and runny honey are delicious.

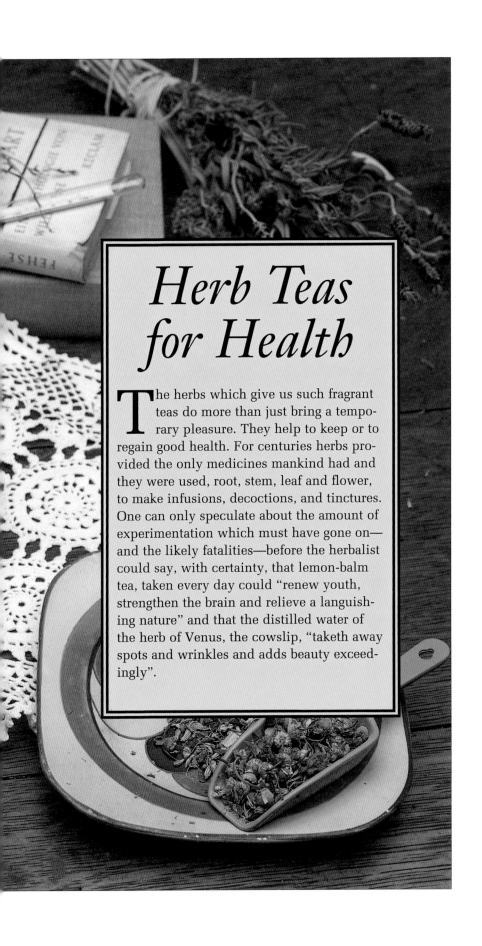

Herb Teas for Health

The herbs which give us such fragrant teas do more than just bring a temporary pleasure. They help to keep or to regain good health. For centuries herbs provided the only medicines mankind had and they were used, root, stem, leaf and flower, to make infusions, decoctions, and tinctures. One can only speculate about the amount of experimentation which must have gone on— and the likely fatalities—before the herbalist could say, with certainty, that lemon-balm tea, taken every day could "renew youth, strengthen the brain and relieve a languishing nature" and that the distilled water of the herb of Venus, the cowslip, "taketh away spots and wrinkles and adds beauty exceedingly".

There are very many more herbs than are mentioned in this little book that can be used medicinally, of course, but they can be considered separately and grown in the garden among other plants or in a special "physick" garden as the monks used to call their collection of herbs used to comfort the sick and strengthen the feeble.

The emphasis here is on how pleasant it is to drink tisanes and it is very nice to find there is at lease one enjoyable thing that will do us good and not harm: sitting cradling a cup in the hands and breathing in the fragrance before the first careful sip is a gentle pleasure. What can be more refreshing than a glass of cold, clear, clean, gold or greenish liquid in which ice tinkles and on which small fresh leaves or flowers are floating?

Many people have an objection to being told to do something which will "do them good"—and one wouldn't want to put anybody off taking herbal tea—but now, having trailed one's coat, so to speak, and established the fun and the pleasure, it is surely safe to stress the benefits.

Ginseng

The root of ginseng has been used medicinally in China for asbout 5,000 years. It is believed to be a cure-all as well as an aphrodisias. A tisane tastes faintly of licorice.

Alfalfa
The roots of alfalfa go deep and bring up trace minerals otherwise inaccessible and make the plant a rich source of iron, magnesium, phosphorous, potassium, sulphur and vitamins A, B12, C, D, E and K. No wonder it makes such a good tonic. It is a good tea to drink after an illness which has required treatment by synthetic drugs—it will clear the body of the accumulated poisons.

Angelica
A good tea to drink if you think a cold is coming on or you feel "rheumaticky".

Basil
When you get the jitters for no apparent reason make a tea from the leaves and the flowering tips— 5g herb to 100g near boiling water and sit quietly and drink it after a meal.

Bergamot
If you make a really strong brew you can use it as a gargle for a sore throat.

54

Borage

The ancients claimed that "borage maketh the mind glad" and since the plant is so rich in mineral salts, potassium and calcium, who's arguing?

A nice cucumber tasting tea made from the leaves and flowers. Will cleanse the blood and liven you up nicely.

Catmint

Tea made from the leaves and flowers can help to sweat out a chill, relieve wind and hiccups, and bring on delayed menstruation. If you have any left in the pot tip in on the flower-bed—it will keep unwanted insects away.

Chamomile

How many have slept more sweetly after a bed-time cup of chamomile tea?

Chamomile tea is one of the great soothers. It eases an upset stomach, quietens nerves and prevents nightmares. It is equally good for children with ear ache or cutting teeth and the harassed parents looking after them.

Lemon Balm

If you have a head-ache and a heavy cold try a tea made from the clean-tasting herb, unsweetened.

Lemon Verbena

The sweetly sharp tasting tea is a help when you have eaten unwisely or too well—and, surprisingly, if you have a stuffy nose or blocked sinuses.

Lovage

A warming drink of lovage tea will deal with stomach wind and is said to help cystitis.

Mint

Mint tea is one of the favourites and is good for the digestion.

Parsley

Parsley makes another tea good for the digestion and the relief of cystitis. Sufferers from menstrual cramps

find it useful too. Tea is made from the leaves—not the seeds.

Rosemary
When nerves are strained and a headache won't go away, try some rosemary tea. It has a long reputation for being able to strengthen the memory.

Sage
Sage tea is good for depression, for sharpening the mental facilities and aiding the memory. It contains oestrogen and will tone up the female reproductive system. It also makes a good gargle for a sore throat.

Solidago (Golden Rod)
The aniseed-flavoured tea was once a favourite for reducing blood pressure and easing inflammation of the mucus membranes.

Thyme
A good "chest" herb and a bracing tonic after 'flu and other debilitating illnesses.

Combination teas to settle the nerves and to promote sleep

For nerves

1. Brew a tea from 1 teaspoon of the following:
>   1 part lemon balm or melissa leaves
>   1 part pepperment leaves
>   2 parts valerian root

Put the valerian root fragments in the cold water, bring to boil, then add the boiling water to the melissa and peppermint leaves, and steep for 5 to 10 minutes.

2. The Agrimonas formula nerve tea is brewed from a teaspoonful of the following mixture per cupful of water; 1 to 2 cups are drunk daily:
>   2g citrus rind
>   3g larkspur flowers
>   2g marigolds
>   2g lavender flowers
>   4g mallow flowers
>   8g lemon balm or melissa leaves
>   5g rosemary leaves
>   8g caraway seeds

12g fennel seeds
8g crampweed or silverweed foliage
2g centaury foliage
17g Saint John's wort foliage
18g peppermint leaves
2g licorice root
2.68g hops

For insomnia
The Kuhne formula tea to relax nerves and combat insomnia is brewed by pouring 1 cupful of boiling water over 1 dessertspoonful of the following mixture, steeping for a few minutes. Drink it before going to bed:
15.5 parts blackberry leaves
3.9 parts strawberry leaves
4.7 parts rose hips (without the seeds)
3.1 parts raspberry leaves
0.4 parts cornflower
1.5 parts linden flowers

What does "real" tea do for you?

Not a lot according to the Encyclopaedia Britanica which says it is mainly a vehicle for large intakes of sugar, milk or lemon and is more appreciated for its effects than its nutritive value.

The effects are well-known—the comfort from the warmth of the steaming brew—the temporary "lift" given by the caffeine it contains.

"I can't get out of bed before I've had my cup of tea". How many people say that! Not for nothing was tea called "the cup that cheers".

I have also seen it referred to as "that windy beverage"—due no doubt to the widespread habit of taking it with milk.

And have you thought about the stain it leaves on the pot?

Tannin is used for tanning leather. What does the tannin in tea do to the stomach walls?

Devoted tea-drinkers will not bother with such questions and who would want to spoil their pleasure by asking them too loudly? But can we not tempt them to experiment just a little, and to find the best of both worlds in the tisanes which taste so pleasant and have such a beneficial effect?

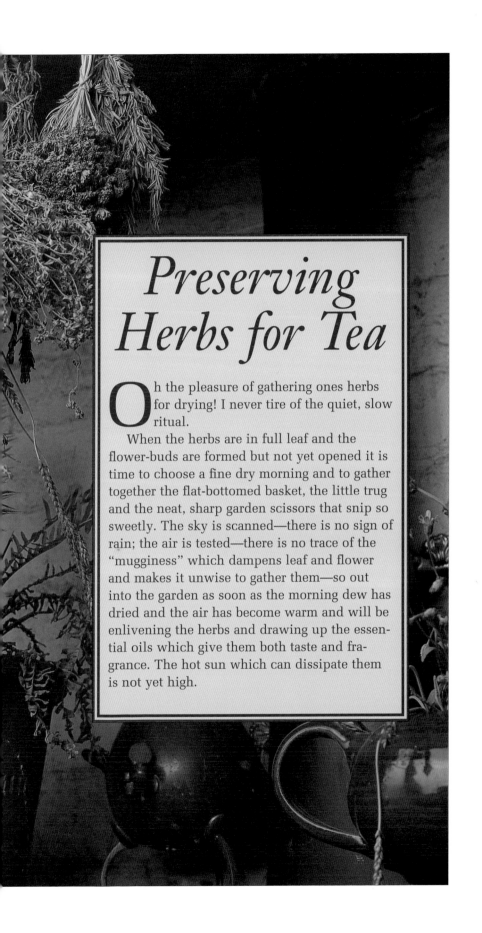

Preserving Herbs for Tea

O h the pleasure of gathering ones herbs for drying! I never tire of the quiet, slow ritual.

When the herbs are in full leaf and the flower-buds are formed but not yet opened it is time to choose a fine dry morning and to gather together the flat-bottomed basket, the little trug and the neat, sharp garden scissors that snip so sweetly. The sky is scanned—there is no sign of rain; the air is tested—there is no trace of the "mugginess" which dampens leaf and flower and makes it unwise to gather them—so out into the garden as soon as the morning dew has dried and the air has become warm and will be enlivening the herbs and drawing up the essential oils which give them both taste and fragrance. The hot sun which can dissipate them is not yet high.

Gathering herbs is a very gentle process. Leaves, stems, flowers, bruise easily and so must be handled lightly. With the left hand facing upward, spread apart the forefinger and second finger of the hand and slide them around the stem to be snipped. Allow the leaves to rest lightly on the fingers. Make the snip and transfer the cut stem to the basket, placing it down carefully so that there is no likelihood of crushing.

Since the herbs begin to lose their vital properties as soon as they are picked it is important not to gather more than can be prepared for drying within a very short time. It helps if there is an accomplice waiting to take on the job while the next picking is being made.

Choosing which herbs to dry and how much of them to use is very much a matter of personal choice. I would never use dried parsley or dried basil for instance. Sauce or tea made with dried parsley seems to have a flat, tired taste, and goodness knows what happens to the flavour of basil.

Drying Herbs

A dry, airy spot out of the sun, protected is what is needed.

A shed with an open door, a room with open windows, but NOT a garage for there are bound to be petrol fumes around. If you are drying on a small scale there should be no problem in finding a place where hooks can be put up and bunches of herbs hung from them. If your kitchen gets steamy—and few don't—try and resist the temptation to have them hanging there, I know they give a nice country atmosphere but they won't dry well.

If you are going in for drying in a bigger way see if you can find of those old fashioned clothes racks, the kind that used to hang in the kitchen and could be let down and drawn up. If you can, find somewhere dry and airy to hang it you will have space to accommodate many bunches at a time.

The more humid the area the smaller and looser the bunches will have to be—the air must be able to flow through the bundle or mould will set in. You can tie a bunch up with string or use a rubber band.

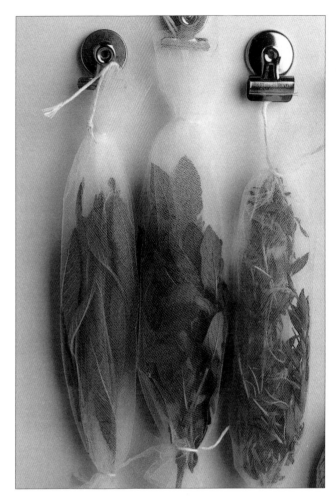

Herbs can be dried in the refrigerator for extra quality and colour. Bundles clipped to magnets which will stick to the inside wall of the fridge.

I like to use string. Tie the stems together, make a loop and hang them head downwards. The loop lets the strung-up bunch dangle more freely than if it is caught up by the rubber band.

If you don't want to hang herbs, you can dry them on the flat. An old well-cleaned fly-screen raised on bricks makes a good base. Cover the screen with a big piece of butter muslin, spread the leaves or flowers over it in a single layer and cover with another piece of muslin and leave for a week or so before inspecting. If you have to use it out of doors it must be put somewhere cool and airy but not cold and blowy and you will have to keep your eyes open for rain.

One of the best dryers I ever had was the childrens' old bunk bed, stripped of its mattresses and left in the spare room. Air circulation was ensured and the drying went very well. Leaves spread out on a large cake rack between two layers of kitchen paper dry quite well too. Some people use newspaper but the ink gives off a vague sort of smell and I prefer the totally odourless and absorbent kitchen roll.

The aim is for the dried herb to keep as much colour and flavour as possible and the sooner drying can begin the better. But loss of moisture should be steady and gradual—a quick frizzle is not recommended. All you'll get is a pile dry, brownish dust.

The leaf should still be green but brittle and easily stripped, whole, from the stem. If it crumbles into bits when you touch it you've overdone it.

Two to three days to a week or more depending on the size and thickness of the material being dried, is the usual time allotted.

But if you want drying to be completed in hours and not days there is always the oven method. This is very popular.

The herbs are spread out in a single layer on paper-covered trays or sheets of very strong paper and put into an oven which is only turned to its lowest heat.

The door must be kept slightly ajar. Most oven doors persist in swinging open so you'll have to find some means of jamming it open to just the right aperture.

You can cover the herbs with some kitchen paper if you wish.

The time needed for drying will be variable, so testing can start after about an hour.

Drying herbs in the microwave oven can work well if the instructions usually to be found in the manufacturers booklet are followed.

The job must be done slowly. If too high a heat is used the herbs will become crisp, brown and tasteless and there is a danger that the volatile oils could combust and set fire to the paper on which the herbs are spread.

To experiment with the microwave, spread the equivalent of a cupful of dry, clean herbs between two plain white paper towels and microwave on high for one minute. Check for dryness, stir or rearrange the herbs, remove any leaves that are already dry, then microwave for another 20 seconds.

The paper towels (at least the bottom one)will probably be wet after the first minute; if so remove the herbs to a dry area of the paper towel before continuing. After every 20-seconds, rearrange the herbs and remove any that are dry. If they get too hot, the herbs will taste scorched.

I know people who swear by the microwave method though.

Is there any difference in the taste of herbs dried by the different methods?

You'll only be able to tell if you test one method against another.

I think there is a difference and have my own preference, but use them all, because sometimes it suits me better to use one way instead of another.

Storing

Conventional wisdom says that dried herbs are not at their best when they have been stored for more than six months and that they should be kept in tightly closed glass jars in a dark cupboard.

It is certainly true about the six months but I think we can take a few liberties about the containers. You can find such pretty little tin ones—such nice little china jars. The temptation to use them is too much to resist. You can keep a 'mother' glass jar in the cupboard and fill up a container to keep on show every now and then. I'm sure the tea won't last long enough to lose its flavour and you will have the pleasure of using something which looks attractive.

Experience does say though that it is better to keep herbs in small containers and to use each one up rather than to keep refilling the same little container from the big storage one, as all that opening and shutting seems to weaken the taste of the herbs in the big jar.

When preparing to fill any container, hold the stems cut side up over a sheet of paper and, with the other hand, stroke gently down the stem to dislodge the leaves. They should come away whole. Make the paper into a funnel and gently transfer tea to the container. Don't press it down too hard—whole leaves keep their taste better than crumbled ones. The time to crumble them is just before the hot water is poured on them.

Index

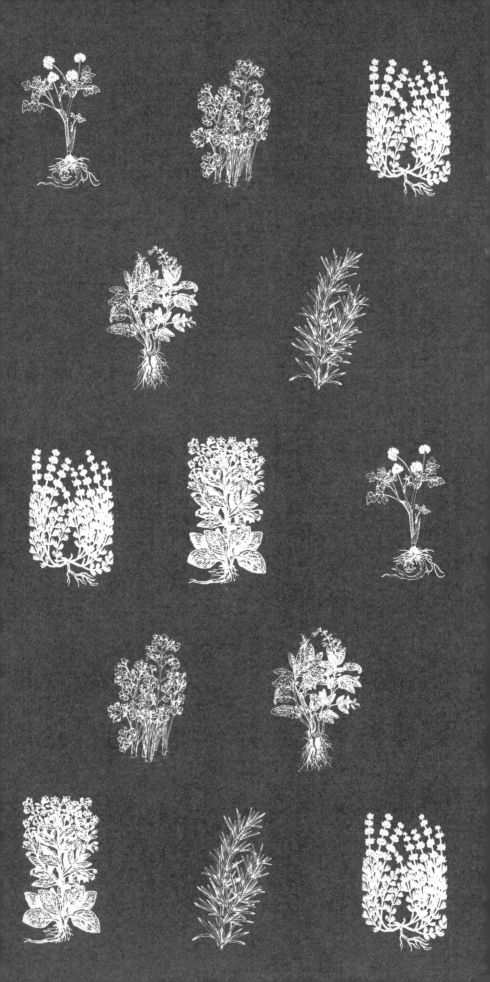